The Interview Code- Crack the Code with Storytelling

Mrigendra Bharti

Published by Sellbrochure Institutions Co., 2024.

While every precaution has been taken in the preparation of this book, the publisher assumes no responsibility for errors or omissions, or for damages resulting from the use of the information contained herein.

THE INTERVIEW CODE- CRACK THE CODE WITH STORYTELLING

First edition. July 26, 2024.

Copyright © 2024 Mrigendra Bharti.

ISBN: 979-8227615008

Written by Mrigendra Bharti.

Table of Contents

Abstract

Crack the Code and Land Your Dream Job: Unveiling the Secrets of Modern Interview Success

The ever-evolving job market demands a dynamic approach to the interview process. "The Interview Code" equips you with the necessary tools and strategies to navigate this competitive landscape and confidently showcase your skills to potential employers. This comprehensive guide unveils the secrets behind three fundamental pillars of interview success: storytelling, virtual interview tactics, and the art of the follow-up email.

Master the art of weaving impactful narratives. Learn how to transform your experiences into compelling stories that resonate with interviewers and effectively communicate your qualifications. This guide dives deep into storytelling techniques, empowering you to craft a captivating narrative that highlights your achievements, problem-solving abilities, and the unique value you bring to the table.

As virtual interviews become increasingly commonplace, "The Interview Code" ensures you're prepared to thrive in this digital environment. Discover practical strategies for presenting yourself professionally and effectively through a screen. From optimizing your background and lighting to mastering nonverbal cues and utilizing technology seamlessly, this guide equips you to make a strong first impression in a virtual setting.

Finally, the power of the follow-up email is not to be underestimated. This guide unveils the secrets of crafting a compelling message that strengthens your candidacy. Learn how to write a concise yet impactful email that reiterates your interest, strategically highlights your qualifications, and leaves a lasting positive impression on the interviewer.

"The Interview Code" extends beyond these core elements, offering comprehensive interview preparation advice. Gain valuable insights into various interview formats, including behavioral, technical, and panel interviews. Additionally, industry-specific considerations are explored, allowing you to tailor your approach to the specific job role and company culture.

This guide is designed for anyone seeking to unlock their full interview potential, from recent graduates and career changers to seasoned professionals looking to take the next step in their journey. By mastering the art of storytelling, conquering the virtual interview, and harnessing the power of the follow-up email, you'll gain the confidence and skills necessary to land your dream job and achieve your career goals.

Chapter 1: Introduction to the Art of Interviewing

Part 1: The Indelible Impact of Effective Interviews

Interviews hold an undeniable power in shaping the course of our lives. They act as gateways to coveted opportunities, propelling us forward in our careers, academic pursuits, and even personal endeavors. From landing your dream job to securing a place at your top-choice university, acing an interview can be the pivotal moment that unlocks a world of possibilities.

The significance of interviews extends far beyond simply acquiring a position or gaining admission. They present a chance to showcase your abilities, articulate your aspirations, and make a lasting impression. A successful interview can be a catalyst for personal growth, boosting your confidence and self-belief. It can open doors to new networks, fostering valuable connections that can enrich your professional journey.

Imagine yourself delivering a compelling response to a challenging interview question. You weave a captivating narrative that exemplifies your skills and experience. The interviewer's eyes light up, and a genuine smile forms on their face. This is the magic of an effective interview. It's not just about providing the right answers; it's about creating a compelling story that convinces the interviewer that you are the perfect fit for the opportunity.

However, the interview landscape can be daunting, especially for those navigating it for the first time. The pressure to perform flawlessly, coupled with the fear of the unknown, can trigger a cascade of anxieties. But fret not! By understanding the interview process, developing a strategic approach, and honing your communication skills, you can transform interview anxiety into a potent source of motivation.

Effective interviews are not merely one-sided interrogations. They are dynamic conversations that allow for a genuine exchange of information. Interviewers seek not only to assess your qualifications but also to gauge your cultural fit, your enthusiasm for the role, and your potential to contribute to their team. By approaching the interview with a spirit of curiosity and engagement, you can not only impress the interviewer but also gain valuable insights into the organization and the opportunity itself.

The impact of a successful interview transcends the immediate outcome. It empowers you with the confidence to tackle future challenges and embrace new opportunities. It equips you with valuable communication skills that can benefit you in diverse aspects of your life, from professional negotiations to personal interactions. Mastering the art of interviewing is an investment in your personal and professional development, yielding dividends for years to come.

Part 2: Demystifying the Interview Landscape

The interview arena encompasses a diverse range of scenarios, each with its own unique set of objectives and expectations. Here, we delve into the three most common interview formats:

* The Job Interview: This is the quintessential interview that most readily springs to mind. It serves as a crucial step in the hiring process, allowing employers to evaluate candidates for specific job openings. Job interviews can be conducted in various formats, including one-on-one interviews, panel interviews, and virtual interviews. The specific format will depend on the organization, the nature of the role, and the stage of the hiring process.

* The Informational Interview: Unlike the job interview, the informational interview is not about securing a position. It's an opportunity to gather information and insights from professionals in your field of interest. This is a valuable tool for career exploration, allowing you to learn about different career paths, gain firsthand knowledge about specific job roles, and build your professional network.

* The Media Interview: If you've ever dreamt of sharing your expertise or perspective on a wider platform, media interviews may be on your horizon. These interviews involve interacting with journalists or media representatives, who will then

disseminate your insights to the public through various channels such as newspapers, magazines, or television broadcasts. Media interviews can be a powerful tool for establishing yourself as a thought leader in your industry and raising your public profile.

Understanding the distinct purposes of these interview formats is paramount. When preparing for a job interview, your focus will be on demonstrating your qualifications and alignment with the specific requirements of the role. In contrast, an informational interview might involve asking targeted questions to gain insights into the day-to-day realities of a particular profession. Similarly, a media interview will necessitate crafting clear, concise, and newsworthy talking points to effectively engage the audience.

Throughout this book, we will delve deeper into the nuances of each interview format, equipping you with the necessary strategies and techniques to excel in any situation. We will explore effective communication methods, answer construction tactics, and essential preparation steps to ensure you approach every interview with confidence and clarity.

Part 3: Taming the Interview Beast: Conquering Interview Anxiety

Butterflies fluttering in your stomach, palms turning clammy, mind going blank – these are all telltale signs of interview anxiety, a common phenomenon that can trip even the most prepared candidate. The very notion of being scrutinized and evaluated can trigger a fight-or-flight response, hindering your ability to perform at your best.

Let's acknowledge that interview anxiety is perfectly normal. It's a natural reaction to a high-pressure situation. However, the key lies in not letting it paralyze you. Here, we will explore effective strategies to manage interview anxiety and transform those nervous jitters into positive energy that fuels your performance.

Acknowledge and Address Your Anxieties:

The first step towards conquering interview anxiety is acknowledging its presence. Don't bottle up your anxieties or berate yourself for feeling nervous. Instead, recognize these anxieties as normal and treatable. Once you acknowledge them, you can begin to develop coping mechanisms.

PREPARATION IS KEY:

One of the most effective antidotes to interview anxiety is thorough preparation. The more prepared you are, the more confident you will feel walking into the interview room. Research the company, the position you are applying for, and common interview questions. Anticipating potential questions allows you to formulate well-structured and insightful answers beforehand.

PRACTICE MAKES PROGRESS:

Rehearsing your responses can significantly boost your confidence. Conduct mock interviews with friends, family, or career counselors. Practice answering common questions out loud, paying attention to your delivery and body language. The more you rehearse, the more comfortable and articulate you will become.

Focus on Your Strengths:

Shift your focus from your anxieties to your strengths and qualifications. Remind yourself of your accomplishments, skills, and the value you bring to the table. Visualize yourself delivering a successful interview, focusing on your positive attributes and capabilities

POSITIVE SELF-TALK:

Challenge negative self-talk with a dose of positivity. Replace thoughts like "I'm going to mess up" with affirmations like "I am prepared" or "I am a strong candidate." Positive self-talk can significantly boost your confidence and emotional resilience.

RELAXATION TECHNIQUES:

Deep breathing exercises and mindfulness techniques can effectively calm your nerves and enhance your focus. Practice deep breathing exercises before the interview to regulate your heart rate and ease anxiety. Mindfulness techniques can help you stay present in the moment and avoid getting overwhelmed by negative thoughts.

Remember, interview anxiety is manageable. By employing these strategies and cultivating a positive mindset, you can transform your interview experience from nerve-wracking to empowering. In the next part of this chapter, we will delve into the foundations you can lay to ensure interview success.

Part 4: Laying the Foundation for Interview Success

Now that we've explored the various interview landscapes and techniques for managing anxiety, let's solidify the groundwork for a triumphant interview experience. Here, we'll discuss the crucial preparatory steps that will bolster your confidence and position you for success.

1. METICULOUS RESEARCH is Your Ally:

* Company Savvy: Invest time in researching the organization you're interviewing with. Understand their mission, values, products or services, and target audience. This knowledge demonstrates your genuine interest and allows you to tailor your responses to their specific needs and goals.

* Industry Insights: Familiarize yourself with current trends and developments within the industry. This showcases your awareness of the bigger picture and how your skills can contribute to the organization's growth.

* Role Clarity: Meticulously examine the job description, pinpointing the key qualifications and desired skills. Analyze how your background aligns with these requirements, and craft examples from your experience that exemplify your suitability for the role.

2. CRAFT A COMPELLING Narrative:

* Storytelling Prowess: Prepare impactful stories that illustrate your skills and experiences using the STAR method (Situation, Task, Action, Result). These narratives should be concise, engaging, and effectively demonstrate your problem-solving abilities and contributions in previous roles.

* Quantify Your Achievements: Whenever possible, quantify your accomplishments with numbers or data. Highlighting measurable results adds credibility to your claims and showcases the tangible impact you can make.

Chapter 2: Mastering the Interview Process

Part 1: Decoding Interview Questions

T he interview room can feel like a minefield of hidden meanings, especially when faced with a barrage of questions. But fear not! Interview questions, while seemingly enigmatic at first glance, often follow a predictable logic. By understanding the different types of questions and the interviewer's underlying motives, you can craft well-structured and insightful answers that effectively showcase your qualifications.

1. UNVEILING THE DIFFERENT Question Types:

* Experience-Based Questions: These questions delve into your past experiences and achievements. They are designed to assess your skills, problem-solving abilities, and how you've handled similar situations in the past. Examples: "Tell me about a time you faced a challenge at work and how you overcame it," or "Describe a situation where you had to work effectively under pressure."

* Behavioral Questions: These questions take experience-based inquiries a step further by focusing on the specific actions you took in a particular scenario. They aim to understand your thought process, decision-making skills, and how you align with the company's values. Examples: "Can you give an example of

a time you demonstrated strong leadership skills?" or "Tell me about a situation where you had to work effectively in a team."

* Situational Questions: These questions present hypothetical scenarios that you might encounter in the role you're applying for. They assess your problem-solving abilities, critical thinking skills, and how you would approach new challenges within the position. Examples: "How would you handle a difficult customer situation?" or "Describe your approach to prioritizing multiple tasks under a tight deadline."

* Technical Questions: These questions are specific to the technical requirements of the job and are designed to evaluate your knowledge and expertise in a particular field. The nature of these questions will vary depending on the industry and role. Examples: "Explain the concept of SEO (Search Engine Optimization)" for a marketing position, or "Describe your experience with coding languages like Java or Python" for a software development role.

---

2. CRACKING THE CODE: Understanding the Interviewer's Intent

Beyond the surface level of questioning, interviewers have a deeper motive. They are not simply seeking factual answers; they are evaluating your potential as a valuable addition to their team. Here's what interviewers are truly trying to understand:

* Skills and Abilities: Can you demonstrate the necessary skills and experience outlined in the job description?

* Problem-Solving Approach: How do you approach challenges and overcome obstacles?

* Communication Skills: Can you articulate your thoughts and ideas clearly and concisely?

* Decision-Making Capabilities: Can you make sound decisions under pressure and with limited information?

* Cultural Fit: Are your values and work style aligned with the company culture?

By keeping these underlying objectives in mind, you can tailor your responses to effectively address the interviewer's concerns.

---

3. CRAFTING STELLAR Answers: A Formula for Success

Here's a practical framework you can utilize to formulate winning answers to interview questions:

* Active Listening: Pay close attention to the question and ensure your response directly addresses the interviewer's intent.

* Highlight Relevant Skills: Connect your response back to the specific skills and experiences mentioned in the job description.

* The STAR Method in Action: Utilize the STAR method (Situation, Task, Action, Result) to structure your stories. Briefly outline the situation, the task at hand, the actions you took, and the positive results you achieved.

* Quantify Whenever Possible: When showcasing your accomplishments, use numbers, data, or metrics to add credibility and demonstrate the impact of your actions.

* Enthusiasm is Key: Deliver your answers with genuine enthusiasm and a positive attitude.

Part 2: Asking Effective Questions: The Art of Two-Way Communication

Interviews are not one-sided interrogations; they are dynamic conversations where both parties have the opportunity to exchange information. While answering the interviewer's questions is crucial, posing thoughtful questions of your own demonstrates genuine interest, initiative, and a well-rounded understanding of the role and organization.

Here's why asking effective questions is a powerful interview strategy:

* Demonstrates Curiosity and Engagement: Well-considered questions showcase your genuine interest in the opportunity and the company culture. It portrays you as someone who is proactive and eager to learn more.

* Reveals Alignment with Company Goals: By asking insightful questions about the team, projects, and company objectives, you demonstrate that you've done your research and are aligned with the organization's values and mission.

* Gains Valuable Insights: The interview is also your chance to gather valuable information about the role, the team dynamics, and the company culture. Asking thoughtful questions allows you to assess if the position and the organization are a good fit for your career aspirations and work style.

Crafting Questions that Impress

Now that we understand the significance of asking questions, let's explore effective strategies for formulating insightful inquiries:

* Beyond the Job Description: While the job description provides a good starting point, delve deeper. Ask questions about specific projects the team is working on, upcoming challenges, or opportunities for professional development within the role.

* Company Culture and Values: Inquire about the company culture, work environment, and core values. This demonstrates your interest in fitting into the team and understanding how the organization operates.

* Growth and Advancement: Ask about opportunities for professional growth, learning and development programs, or mentorship opportunities within the company. This showcases your ambition and desire to learn and contribute in the long term.

EXAMPLES OF EFFECTIVE Questions:

* "Can you elaborate on a typical day or week in this role?"

* "What are some of the biggest challenges and opportunities facing the team currently?"

* "How does this position contribute to the overall goals of the company?"

* "What are the company's expectations for someone hired in this role in the first 90 days?"

* "What professional development opportunities does the company offer to its employees?"

Remember, the quality of your questions is just as important as the quantity. By asking thoughtful and insightful questions, you position yourself as a proactive and engaged candidate who is genuinely interested in the opportunity.

Part 3: Engaging in Meaningful Conversations: The Power of Rapport Building

Imagine an interview that transcends the typical question-and-answer format. Instead, it unfolds as a natural and engaging conversation where both parties actively listen, share ideas, and build a sense of rapport. This is the power of an interview focused on meaningful conversation, a strategy that can significantly enhance your chances of landing the job.

WHY RAPPORT MATTERS

Rapport is that intangible connection that fosters trust, understanding, and a sense of mutual respect. By establishing rapport with the interviewer, you create a more positive and relaxed atmosphere. This allows you to showcase your personality, communication skills, and ability to connect with others – all essential qualities for success in any professional setting.

BUILDING BRIDGES OF Rapport

Here are some key strategies to cultivate rapport during your interview:

* Confident and Positive Body Language: Maintain good posture, make eye contact, and offer a genuine smile. Project an air of confidence and enthusiasm throughout the conversation.

* Active Listening: Pay close attention to the interviewer's questions and responses. Ask clarifying questions to demonstrate your understanding and engagement

* Mirroring and Matching: Subtly mirror the interviewer's communication style, energy level, and even body language (within reason) to create a sense of connection.

* Finding Common Ground: Look for opportunities to find common interests or experiences you share with the interviewer. This can create a sense of familiarity and ease conversation flow.

* Enthusiasm is Contagious: Express genuine enthusiasm for the opportunity and the company. Your excitement will be palpable and can leave a positive impression on the interviewer.

CONVERSATIONAL INTELLIGENCE

Beyond technical skills and experience, employers often seek candidates who possess strong emotional intelligence and the ability to connect with others. Demonstrating your conversational prowess during the interview allows you to showcase these valuable qualities.

* Storytelling as a Tool: Weave relevant stories and anecdotes into your responses to illustrate your points and create a more engaging conversation.

* Respond with Questions: Don't just answer questions; ask follow-up questions to demonstrate your curiosity and keep the conversation flowing naturally.

* Positive Language: Use positive and enthusiastic language throughout the interview. Avoid negativity or complaining, even when discussing past challenges.

Remember, the interview is a two-way street. By focusing on building rapport and engaging in meaningful conversation, you create a more positive and memorable experience for both yourself and the interviewer. This approach can significantly increase your chances of landing the job and starting a successful new chapter in your career.

Part 4: Handling Challenging Situations: Grace Under Pressure

Interviews, while ideally smooth and flowing conversations, can sometimes veer into unexpected territory. You may encounter challenging questions, awkward silences, or even technical difficulties. Here's how to navigate these situations with composure and maintain a positive impression:

1. THE CURVEBALL QUESTION:

Sometimes, interviewers may throw you a curveball question – something unexpected or beyond the scope of your prepared responses. Don't panic! Take a deep breath and employ these strategies:

* Acknowledge and Clarify: Acknowledge that the question is unexpected and politely ask for clarification if needed. This demonstrates your composure and desire to understand the question fully.

* Relate it Back: If possible, try to connect the unexpected question back to your skills and experiences. Briefly showcase how your qualifications can be applied to address the situation presented in the question.

* Honesty is Key: If you genuinely don't know the answer, be honest. You can explain that you haven't encountered this

specific situation before, but you are a quick learner and eager to tackle new challenges.

---

2. THE UNCOMFORTABLE Silence:

Uncomfortable silences can be nerve-wracking, but they don't have to derail your interview. Here's how to handle them:

* Pause and Compose Yourself: Don't feel pressured to fill the silence immediately. Take a moment to gather your thoughts and formulate a well-constructed response.

* Elaborate on Your Answer: If you've just finished answering a question, consider elaborating with additional details or insights to prevent an awkward pause.

* Ask a Clarifying Question: If the silence persists, politely ask a clarifying question related to the previous topic to restart the conversation.

---

3. TECHNICAL GLITCHES and Disruptions:

In the age of virtual interviews, technical difficulties are a possibility. Here's how to manage them:

* Maintain Composure: Stay calm and professional if you encounter technical issues like internet connection problems or audio disruptions.

* Communicate Clearly: Inform the interviewer of the technical difficulty and ask for their patience while you try to resolve it.

* Be Prepared with a Backup Plan: If possible, have a backup phone or internet connection available in case of technical glitches.

Remember, even challenging situations can be opportunities to showcase your composure, problem-solving skills, and adaptability. By remaining calm, professional, and resourceful, you can navigate these hurdles and leave a positive lasting impression on the interviewer.

This concludes Chapter 2 on Mastering the Interview Process. In the next chapter, we'll delve into the art of storytelling in interviews, a powerful tool to captivate your audience and make your responses truly memorable.

Chapter 3: The Art of Storytelling in Interviews

Part 1: The Power of Storytelling

The human brain is wired for stories. We are naturally drawn to narratives that capture our imagination, evoke emotions, and convey information in a compelling manner. Interviews, while often perceived as dry exchanges of questions and answers, present a golden opportunity to harness the power of storytelling. By incorporating well-crafted narratives into your responses, you can transform your interview from a monotonous recitation of skills to a captivating performance that showcases your personality, experiences, and value proposition.

WHY STORIES WORK

Stories serve several crucial functions in an interview setting:

* Engaging Your Audience: Stories have the power to capture the interviewer's attention and hold their interest. They create a sense of connection and make your responses more memorable than a simple list of qualifications.

* Illustrating Your Skills: Facts and figures are important, but stories breathe life into them. By weaving anecdotes into your responses, you can demonstrate how you applied your skills in real-world situations and achieved tangible results.

* Showcasing Your Personality: Stories offer a window into your personality, values, and thought processes. They reveal how you

approach challenges, overcome obstacles, and collaborate with others.

* Emotional Connection: Stories have the power to evoke emotions in the listener. By incorporating an emotional element into your narratives, you can create a deeper connection with the interviewer and leave a lasting impression.

The STAR Method: A Storytelling Framework

To ensure your stories are impactful and effectively showcase your skills, consider utilizing the STAR method:

* Situation: Briefly describe the context or scenario you faced.

* Task: Outline the specific task or challenge you were responsible for addressing.

* Action: Detail the actions you took to address the situation and overcome the challenge.

* Result: Highlight the positive outcome of your actions and the impact you made.

Part 2: Crafting Your Interview Narratives

Now that we've explored the power of storytelling in interviews and the STAR method as a structuring framework, let's delve into the practical steps of crafting compelling interview narratives.

1. IDENTIFYING RELEVANT Stories:

Not all experiences deserve a place in your interview narrative arsenal. Here's how to identify stories that resonate with the specific role you're applying for:

* Review the Job Description: The job description serves as a roadmap for your interview stories. Identify the key skills and experiences mentioned, and brainstorm stories that exemplify your proficiency in those areas.

* Reflect on Your Accomplishments: Think back on successes and challenges you've encountered in previous roles or projects. Consider how these experiences showcase the skills and qualities valued by the company you're interviewing with.

* Variety is Key: While focusing on relevant skills, don't limit yourself to a single story type. Aim for a diverse repertoire of narratives that demonstrate different facets of your capabilities and personality.

2. TAILORING YOUR STORIES:

A one-size-fits-all approach to interview stories won't suffice. Here's how to tailor your narratives to resonate with the specific interview and opportunity:

* Highlight Alignments: Connect your stories back to the specific requirements and challenges mentioned in the job description. Illustrate how your past experiences equip you to excel in this particular role.

* Company Culture Fit: If you've researched the company culture, consider incorporating stories that reflect values or approaches similar to those of the organization. This demonstrates your understanding of their culture and potential fit within the team.

* Focus on Impact: The core of every compelling story is the impact you made. Ensure your narratives highlight the positive results and value you delivered through your actions.

3. REFINING YOUR DELIVERY:

The delivery of your stories is just as important as the content itself. Here's how to ensure your narratives are engaging and impactful

* Clarity and Concision: Avoid rambling or going off on tangents. Present your stories in a clear, concise, and well-structured manner.

* Enthusiasm is Contagious: Deliver your stories with genuine enthusiasm and conviction. Your passion for your experiences will resonate with the interviewer and leave a lasting impression.

* Vocal Variety: Use vocal variety to keep the listener engaged. Modulate your voice, vary your pacing, and add emphasis when necessary to bring your story to life.

* Body Language Matters: Maintain good eye contact, use natural gestures, and project confident body language while sharing your stories. This enhances your credibility and reinforces your message.

Part 3: Delivering Impactful Stories: Mastering the Art of Presentation

You've identified compelling stories, tailored them to the specific interview, and honed your delivery – now it's time to unleash the power of storytelling in the interview room. Here's how to captivate your audience and deliver your narratives with confidence and poise.

1. CONFIDENCE IS KEY:

Projecting confidence is paramount when presenting your stories. Here are some confidence-boosting strategies:

* Practice Makes Perfect: Rehearse your stories beforehand, paying attention to your delivery and body language. This practice builds muscle memory and increases your comfort level.

* Positive Self-Talk: Challenge negative self-doubt with positive affirmations. Remind yourself of your accomplishments and the value you bring to the table

* Visualize Success: Before the interview, take a few moments to visualize yourself delivering your stories with clarity and confidence. This mental rehearsal can significantly boost your confidence in the moment.

2. ENGAGING YOUR AUDIENCE:

The goal is not just to tell your story; it's to capture the interviewer's attention and make them invested in your narrative. Here are some techniques to achieve that:

* Start Strong: Hook the interviewer from the beginning with a strong opening line or anecdote that sets the stage for your story.

* Vivid Details: Paint a picture with your words. Use sensory details to create a vivid experience for the listener and bring your story to life.

* Emotional Connection: While maintaining professionalism, don't be afraid to inject a touch of emotion into your stories. Authenticity and passion can resonate with the interviewer and create a deeper connection.

* Maintain Eye Contact: Make eye contact with the interviewer throughout your story. This demonstrates confidence, engagement, and sincerity.

---

3. THE POWER OF PAUSING:

Effective silence can be a powerful tool in storytelling. Here's how to utilize pauses strategically:

* Emphasis and Impact: After delivering a key point in your story, utilize a pause to allow the impact to sink in for the interviewer.

* Building Anticipation: A well-timed pause before revealing the outcome of your story can build anticipation and keep the interviewer engaged.

* Composure and Control: Pausing also demonstrates composure and control over the interview narrative. Don't feel pressured to fill every silence with words.

---

4. ENDING ON A HIGH Note:

Leave a lasting impression by concluding your story with a strong closing statement. Briefly summarize the key takeaway and reiterate the value you delivered.

By mastering the art of storytelling and delivering your narratives with confidence and engagement, you can transform your interview from a series of questions and answers into a captivating performance that showcases your abilities, experiences, and potential as a valuable asset to the organization.

Part 4: Beyond the Basics: Advanced Storytelling Techniques

While the core principles of storytelling remain constant, there are advanced techniques you can employ to elevate your interview narratives to the next level. Here, we'll explore some strategies for crafting truly exceptional stories that will leave a lasting impression on the interviewer.

1. THE HERO'S JOURNEY:

The Hero's Journey, a storytelling archetype found in myths and narratives across cultures, can be a powerful framework for structuring your interview stories. This framework outlines a common narrative structure with these key stages:

* The Ordinary World: Briefly introduce yourself and your background, setting the stage for the challenge you faced.

* The Call to Adventure: Describe the situation or problem that presented itself, prompting you to take action.

* Refusal of the Call (Optional): You can briefly mention any initial hesitations or doubts you had before taking on the challenge.

* Meeting the Mentor: Highlight the guidance or support you received from a colleague, supervisor, or resource that helped you address the challenge.

* Crossing the Threshold: Describe your initial steps towards tackling the challenge and venturing into unfamiliar territory.

* Tests, Allies, and Enemies: Outline the obstacles you encountered, the people who supported you, and any challenges you had to overcome.

* Approach to the Innermost Cave: Describe the key moment or turning point where you devised a solution or overcame a significant hurdle.

* The Ordeal: Detail the most significant challenge or obstacle you faced in overcoming the situation.

* Reward (The Result): Highlight the positive outcome of your actions and the value you delivered.

* The Road Back: Briefly mention how the experience or accomplishment impacted you and your approach to future challenges.

* Resurrection: Describe how you applied the lessons learned from this experience in a future situation.

* Return with the Elixir: Conclude your story by reiterating the key skills or qualities you gained from this experience and how they make you a valuable asset to the company.

By incorporating this framework, you can create compelling interview narratives that showcase your problem-solving skills, resilience, and ability to overcome challenges – all qualities highly sought-after by employers.

---

2. THE EMOTIONAL ARC

Stories rarely exist in a vacuum of pure facts and figures. Emotions play a crucial role in connecting with the listener and creating a memorable narrative. Here's how to incorporate an emotional arc into your interview stories

* Start with a relatable emotion: Begin your story by setting the emotional stage. Perhaps you felt frustrated with the existing system, overwhelmed by the challenge, or excited about the opportunity to make a difference.

* Building Tension: As your story progresses, gradually build tension by describing the obstacles you faced and the potential consequences of failure.

* The Climax and Resolution: The climax of your story should be the moment of greatest challenge or tension. Here, highlight the actions you took and the emotional shift that occurred as you overcame the obstacle.

* End on a Positive Note: Conclude your story with a sense of accomplishment, satisfaction, or hope. This leaves a positive impression on the interviewer and reinforces the value you delivered.

3. SHOW, DON'T TELL

Stories are most impactful when they allow the listener to experience the events firsthand. Here's how to utilize "show, don't tell" in your interview narratives:

* Focus on Action and Dialogue: Instead of simply stating your problem-solving skills, showcase them in action by describing specific steps you took and conversations you had with colleagues or clients

* Sensory Details: Engage the interviewer's senses by incorporating vivid details related to sight, sound, smell, touch, and even taste (if relevant) to bring your story to life.

* Figurative Language: Use metaphors, similes, and other figures of speech sparingly to add depth and create a more captivating narrative.

By incorporating these advanced techniques, you can elevate your storytelling to a whole new level, transforming your interview responses into powerful and memorable narratives that showcase your unique value proposition and leave a lasting impression on the interviewer.

This concludes Chapter 3 on the Art of Storytelling in Interviews. In the next chapter, we'll delve into the specific considerations for successful virtual interviews, ensuring you present yourself professionally and effectively in an online setting.

Chapter 4: Conquering the Virtual Interview Landscape

Part 1: Preparing for the Virtual Interview

Just like an in-person interview, meticulous preparation is paramount for virtual success. Here are some key steps to take before your virtual interview:

1. TECHNOLOGY CHECK and Backup Plan:

* Reliable Technology: Ensure you have a stable internet connection, a functioning webcam, and a high-quality microphone. Test your equipment beforehand and have backup options ready in case of technical glitches.

* Software Familiarity: Familiarize yourself with the video conferencing platform being used for the interview. Practice logging in, navigating the interface, and ensuring your audio and video settings are optimized.

* Professional Background: Choose a quiet, well-lit space for your interview. Ensure the background is clutter-free and professional – a simple, solid-colored backdrop is ideal.

2. DRESS FOR SUCCESS (Even Virtually):

First impressions matter, even in a virtual setting. Dress professionally for your interview, just as you would for an in-person meeting. Attire that reflects the company culture and the position you're applying for demonstrates respect and seriousness about the opportunity.

---

3. PRACTICE MAKES PERFECT:

Just like you would for an in-person interview, conduct mock interviews virtually. Utilize video conferencing platforms to rehearse your responses, ensuring your body language and communication style translate well online. Consider practicing with a friend or family member, or utilize online interview simulation tools.

---

4. PREPARE YOUR TALKING Points:

While the physical interview space may be different, the need for preparation remains crucial. Have your interview notes, talking points, and a list of potential questions readily accessible on your computer for easy reference during the virtual meeting.

Part 2: Mastering the Virtual Interview Experience

With meticulous preparation under your belt, let's delve into the nitty-gritty of navigating the virtual interview itself. Here are some key strategies to ensure you present yourself professionally and effectively in the online environment:

1. MINIMIZE DISTRACTIONS:

* Silence Your Surroundings: Inform anyone in your household about the interview and ensure the environment is quiet and free from disruptions. Turn off your phone notifications and silence any other potential noisemakers.

* Professional Demeanor: Maintain a professional demeanor throughout the interview. Avoid multitasking, checking emails, or engaging in any activities that could detract from your focus and attentiveness.

2. MIND YOUR BODY LANGUAGE and Non-Verbal Cues:

* Eye Contact is Key: Maintain good eye contact with the interviewer by looking directly into the webcam. This conveys attentiveness, confidence, and genuine interest in the conversation.

* Posture Matters: Sit up straight and maintain good posture throughout the interview. This projects professionalism, confidence, and engagement.

* Avoid Distracting Gestures: Be mindful of your body language and avoid fidgeting, excessive leaning, or distracting hand gestures that can come across as unprofessional in a virtual setting.

3. SPEAK CLEARLY AND Project Your Voice:

* Clear Communication: Enunciate clearly and speak at a moderate pace. Being mindful of your microphone volume ensures the interviewer can hear you clearly.

* Minimize Background Noise: Use headphones with a microphone to minimize background noise and improve audio quality.

4. EMBRACE THE POWER of Pauses:

In a virtual setting, there may be slight audio or video delays. Utilize pauses strategically to avoid interrupting the interviewer and allow for clear communication. Don't be afraid to take a beat to gather your thoughts before responding to a question.

5. LEVERAGE THE CHAT Function (if available):

Some video conferencing platforms offer a chat function. Utilize this feature strategically, if permitted, to share documents, websites, or links relevant to the conversation without interrupting the interview flow.

---

6. FOLLOWING UP IS Essential:

Even after a virtual interview, a follow-up thank-you email is essential. Thank the interviewer for their time and reiterate your interest in the position. Briefly mention a specific point discussed in the interview to showcase your attentiveness and continued enthusiasm for the opportunity.

By following these strategies and maintaining a professional and engaged demeanor, you can conquer the virtual interview landscape and make a strong impression on potential employers, increasing your chances of landing your dream job.

In the next part of this chapter, we'll explore additional considerations specific to different virtual interview formats, such as pre-recorded interviews and one-way video interviews.

Part 3: Adapting to Different Virtual Interview Formats

The virtual interview landscape encompasses various formats beyond the traditional live video call. Here's how to excel in some of the more common alternative interview formats:

1. PRE-RECORDED VIDEO Interviews:

Some companies utilize pre-recorded video interviews as an initial screening stage. Here's how to approach them effectively:

* Practice Makes Perfect: Since you won't have the opportunity for real-time interaction, practice your responses beforehand. Pay attention to pacing, clarity, and maintaining a natural conversational tone.

* Lighting and Background: Ensure proper lighting and a professional background just as you would for a live video interview. Dress professionally and maintain good posture throughout the recording.

* Time Management: Pay close attention to time limits for each question. If possible, practice beforehand to ensure you can deliver concise and impactful responses within the allocated timeframe.

2. ONE-WAY VIDEO INTERVIEWS:

One-way video interviews involve recording yourself answering a set of pre-determined questions. Here are some strategies for success:

* Research the Questions: If possible, try to research the types of questions that might be asked beforehand. This allows you to prepare thoughtful and relevant responses.

* Script as a Guide (Not a Crutch): Consider creating a script as a guide for your responses, but avoid sounding scripted or robotic during the recording. Speak naturally and inject your personality into your answers.

* Multiple Takes: Most one-way video interview platforms allow for multiple takes. Utilize this feature to your advantage and re-record responses if you stumble or feel you can improve your delivery.

3. GROUP VIDEO INTERVIEWS:

Group video interviews can be a dynamic way for employers to assess your communication and collaboration skills. Here's how to shine in a virtual group setting:

* Arrive Early (Virtually): Log in to the video conference a few minutes early to avoid technical difficulties and ensure you don't miss any introductions.

* Be Mindful of Others: While it's important to be assertive and showcase your qualifications, be mindful of interrupting others in the group. Wait for pauses in the conversation and use verbal cues like "may I add something?" to interject politely.

* Non-Verbal Cues: Maintain good eye contact and use nonverbal cues like nodding to acknowledge others' points and project an engaged demeanor throughout the interview.

By understanding the nuances of these different virtual interview formats and adapting your approach accordingly, you can demonstrate your versatility and professionalism in any online interview setting.

Remember, effective preparation, a positive attitude, and strong communication skills are key to success in any interview format. This concludes Chapter 4 on Conquering the Virtual Interview Landscape. In the next chapter, we'll provide a comprehensive guide to crafting a compelling follow-up email after your interview.

Chapter 5: The Art of the Follow-Up: Sealing the Deal

$\left(\mathbf{P}^{\text{art 1}}\right)$

The interview is over. You've presented yourself, answered questions, and hopefully, left a positive impression on the interviewer. But the job isn't done yet. In today's competitive job market, the follow-up email after an interview plays a crucial role in solidifying your candidacy and demonstrating your continued interest in the opportunity.

WHY THE FOLLOW-UP MATTERS

You might be thinking, "Didn't I already express my interest during the interview?" While the interview is certainly your primary platform to showcase your qualifications and enthusiasm, a well-crafted follow-up email serves several key purposes:

* Reiterate Your Interest: The interview process often involves multiple candidates. A timely and well-written follow-up email reminds the interviewer of your candidacy and reinforces your genuine interest in the position.

* Highlight Key Points: During the interview, there may have been specific details about your skills or experiences you wanted to emphasize. The follow-up email allows you to subtly reiterate these key points and ensure they stay top-of-mind for the interviewer.

* Demonstrate Professionalism: A thoughtful and well-written follow-up email showcases your professionalism, attention to

detail, and communication skills – all valuable attributes for any potential employer.

* Open the Door for Further Communication: The follow-up email can be used to address any questions you may have forgotten to ask during the interview or to provide additional information that strengthens your candidacy.

In short, the follow-up email is not just a courtesy; it's a strategic opportunity to make a lasting positive impression and potentially differentiate yourself from other candidates.

THE NEXT STEPS: CRAFTING Your Follow-Up Message

Now that we understand the significance of the follow-up email, let's delve into the nitty-gritty of crafting a compelling message. In the next part of this chapter, we'll explore the key elements of a powerful follow-up email structure, ensuring your message resonates with the interviewer and positions you for success in the final stages of the interview process.

(Part 2)

Crafting Your Follow-Up Message: A Strategic Structure

A well-structured follow-up email should be concise, informative, and leave a positive lasting impression. Here's a framework to guide you in crafting your message:

———

1. THE TIMELY SALUTATION:

* Promptness is Key: Aim to send your follow-up email within 24 hours of the interview while the conversation is still fresh in the interviewer's mind.

* Get it Right: Address the email to the interviewer by name, ideally using the same title or salutation they used during the interview (e.g., Mr., Ms., Dr., etc.).

———

2. A PERSONALIZED GREETING:

* Beyond "Dear Sir/Madam": A generic salutation can feel impersonal. If you can't recall the interviewer's name, reference the specific job title or department you interviewed for.

* Expressing Gratitude: Begin your email by thanking the interviewer for their time and consideration during the interview.

———

3. REITERATE YOUR INTEREST:

* Enthusiasm is Contagious: Express your continued enthusiasm for the opportunity and the company. Briefly mention what excites you about the role and how your skills and experience align with the position's requirements.

---

4. HIGHLIGHTING KEY Points:

* Subtle Reinforcement: Subtly highlight a specific point or topic discussed during the interview that showcases your qualifications or experience relevant to the role.

* Offer Additional Information (Optional): If you have any additional information that strengthens your candidacy, such as a relevant work sample or project you forgot to mention, briefly mention it here and offer to share it.

---

5. CLOSING AND CALL to Action:

* Professional Closing: Conclude your email with a professional closing like "Sincerely," "Thank you again," or "Best regards."

* Open the Door for Next Steps: Subtly express your availability for further discussion and reiterate your interest in moving forward in the interview process.

Here's an example of how you can incorporate these elements into your follow-up email:

> SUBJECT: THANK YOU - [Your Name] - [Job Title] Interview

>

Dear [Interviewer Name],

Thank you very much for taking the time to interview me for the [Job Title] position yesterday. I enjoyed learning more about the role and [Company Name]'s exciting work in [Industry].

The discussion about [Specific topic discussed] further solidified my interest in the position. My experience in [Your relevant experience] aligns perfectly with the requirements you outlined, and I am confident I can make a significant contribution to your team.

I particularly enjoyed learning more about [Something specific you found interesting about the company or role]. My passion for [Your relevant skill or area of expertise] aligns perfectly with [Company Name]'s commitment to [Company value].

I have attached [Optional: Relevant work sample or additional information] for your reference, and I am happy to provide any further details you may require.

Thank you again for your time and consideration. I look forward to hearing from you soon regarding the next steps in the interview process.

Sincerely,

[Your Name]

REMEMBER, PROOFREAD your email meticulously before sending it to eliminate any typos or grammatical errors. A polished and professional follow-up email can make a significant difference in your candidacy.

In the next part of this chapter, we'll explore some additional tips for maximizing the impact of your follow-up email.

(Part 3)

Maximizing the Impact of Your Follow-Up Email: Additional Tips

Crafting a well-structured follow-up email is crucial, but there are additional steps you can take to ensure your message resonates with the interviewer:

* Personalize When Possible: If you interacted with anyone else during the interview process, like an HR representative, consider sending a separate brief thank-you email acknowledging their time as well.

* Keep it Concise: Aim for a concise email, ideally within 3-4 paragraphs. The interviewer's time is valuable; get straight to the point while expressing your appreciation and enthusiasm.

* Proofread and Edit: Typos and grammatical errors can leave a negative impression. Proofread your email meticulously before sending it. Consider having someone else review it for any oversights.

* Follow Up (Respectfully): If you haven't heard back within a reasonable timeframe (usually within a week), a polite follow-up email is acceptable. Briefly reiterate your interest and inquire about the next steps in the process

* Avoid Excessive Follow-Ups: While persistence is admirable, sending multiple follow-up emails within a short period can come across as pushy. If you don't hear back after two respectful follow-up attempts, it's best to move on.

Beyond the Email: Additional Considerations

The follow-up process can extend beyond the email. Here are some additional points to consider:

* A Thank-You Note (Optional): While emails are the norm, if you interviewed in a more traditional setting, consider sending a handwritten thank-you note to the interviewer. This can add a personal touch and demonstrate your attention to detail.

* Stay Connected (Professionally): If the interview process doesn't lead to an offer, consider staying connected with the company on social media (LinkedIn) or through their company newsletter. This demonstrates your continued interest and could lead to future opportunities.

By following these strategies and crafting a compelling follow-up email, you can ensure your candidacy stays top-of-mind with the interviewer and increase your chances of landing your dream job.

This concludes Chapter 5 on The Art of the Follow-Up: Sealing the Deal. We hope this comprehensive guide empowers you to excel in your job search and leave a lasting positive impression throughout the interview process.

In Conclusion: Mastering the Interview Process

Congratulations! You've reached the end of this comprehensive guide to mastering the interview process. This guide has equipped you with valuable strategies for crafting compelling stories, excelling in virtual interview settings, and leaving a lasting positive impression with your follow-up email.

Remember, a successful interview is a two-way street. While showcasing your skills and experience is crucial, actively engage with the interviewer, ask insightful questions, and demonstrate your genuine interest in the opportunity. By combining these elements with the strategies outlined in this guide, you can approach your next interview with confidence and position yourself for success.

We wish you all the best in your job search!

About the Author

Mrigendra Bharti, born on June 29, 2004, in South Delhi, India, is a multifaceted individual recognized as the owner of Mrigendra Bharti Group InfoTech India Co. Pvt Ltd. Beyond his entrepreneurial endeavors, he is a distinguished music producer, director, and a budding writer.

Embarking on his professional journey at a young age, Mrigendra Bharti's visionary leadership has led to the establishment of several successful ventures, including Croma Music Series Entertainment, Sellbrochure, Fauget Innovative, and more.

What sets Mrigendra apart is his early initiation into the world of business. His foray into the unknown realms of entrepreneurship began during his 10th-grade years, where he delved into the music industry. This initial venture laid the foundation for subsequent achievements, showcasing his dedication and resilience.

Having honed his skills in music, Mrigendra Bharti not only demonstrated significant growth in his craft but also expanded his professional network. His passion extends beyond music, encompassing app and website development, as well as graphic design.

Fueled by his creative aspirations, Mrigendra established the Mrigendra Bharti Group, a company specializing in website and app development. Currently, he collaborates with a dedicated team, collectively working on ambitious projects that promise innovation and excellence.

Mrigendra's journey serves as an inspiration, particularly for today's students, highlighting the potential of youthful determination and the ability to transform innovative ideas into successful businesses. As he continues to make strides in various domains, Mrigendra Bharti remains a dynamic force, contributing vibrancy to the realms of business, music, and technology.

Read more at https://www.imwriter-mrigendra.rf.gd.